DUNCAN HALLAS

THE GREAT REVOLUTIONS

a Redwords pamphlet

The Great Revolutionns
articles from *Socialist Worker* by Duncan Hallas
Introduction by John Rudge

A Redwords pamphlet published April 2024

ISBN: 978-1-917020-05-3

Redwords is connected to
Bookmarks: The Socialist Bookshop,
1 Bloomsbury Street, London WC1B 3QE
https://bookmarksbookshop.co.uk

Design and production: Roger Huddle
Printed by Halstan & Co. Ltd.

Duncan Hallas, was a revolutionary Marxist, a leading member of the Socialist Workers Party, speaker and teacher; born 23 December 1925, died 19 September 2002.

CONTENTS

    Introduction | 7

1: Men of property against the King | 09

2: Civil war, then compromise | 14

3: Revolt by 'colonials' that launched the USA | 19

4: 'Terrible ones' take up arms | 24

5: Equality – but only for the few | 30

6: Turning point: 1848 – the workers come onto the stage | 35

7: 1871: The first workers' state | 41

8: Dress rehearsal for October | 46

9: Russia on the brink | 51

10: Red October! | 56

Originally printed in Socialist Worker *between September and December 1973*

6

INTRODUCTION
John Rudge

DUNCAN HALLAS* (1925-2002) was one of the thirty-three founding members of the Socialist Review Group, the forerunner of the International Socialists and the Socialist Workers Party. His contributions to the movement over a lifetime of active involvement were vast and covered the fields of theory, propaganda and action.

Duncan was one of the Party's most popular speakers and his enormous output of written contributions were always a joy to read – packed with politics that were delivered in a thoroughly understandable yet serious manner. He may have been a school teacher by training and profession but he was a true educator in the very broadest sense of the word.

During the latter part of 1973 Duncan wrote an 'important new series' of articles under the title 'The Great Revolutions'. They appeared in ten separate parts in *Socialist Worker* between 8th September and 8th December 1973. They count as possibly the greatest lost gems amongst his writings as none of the ten articles has been seen since and, indeed, to date, none of them has even appeared on Duncan's Marxist Internet Archive page.

Duncan takes the reader though both bourgeois and worker revolutions – the English Revolution, the American Revolution, the French Revolution, the 'turning point' revolutionary year of 1848, the Paris Commune and the Russian Revolutions of 1905 and 1917 – in a way that is thoroughly compelling. As you come to the end of each article you cannot help but to want to immediately read what comes next.

Each article in the series is a marvellous piece in its own right and is dripping with those special attributes that

---

* For more on Duncan's life, political contributions and a selected bibliography of his works the reader should consult *Duncan Hallas: Indomitable Revolutionary,* published by Bookmarks in 2023.

made Duncan such an inspiring writer – providing in a weekly agitational newspaper, widely read by workers, politics that were serious, instructive and wholly relevant to his audience. Taken together the articles form a cohesive whole whose simple yet elegant prose combined with deep political insight add significantly to our knowledge and understanding of revolution and the revolutionary process. Seldom has the phrase 'the whole is greater than the sum of its parts' been more apt.

Such was the popularity of Duncan's series at the time of original publication that *Socialist Worker,* 8 December 1973, announced alongside the tenth and final installment that 'The Great Revolutions' series would appear as a pamphlet the following year.

In the event a host of other issues and priorities overtook the International Socialists in 1974 and the pamphlet never appeared.

At the fifieth anniversary of their original publication, it seems appropriate to right that wrong and finally make these important and inspiring writings by one of the great figures of the Socialist Workers Party available once more.

October, 2023

Part 1 :
MEN OF PROPERTY AGAINST THE KING

'EVERY CONSTITUTION RESTS UPON A REVOLUTION.' The British constitution is no exception. It was the English and Scottish revolutions of the seventeenth century that swept away the political obstacles to the development of capitalism in Britain. They laid the basis for the whole set of laws, conventions and political institutions needed for the running of capitalism and which together make up the 'constitution'.

It could not have happened in any other way. For centuries the old feudal order had been decaying and money, trade and manufactures (not yet in factories) had been becoming more and more important. So too had the merchants and capitalist landlords who controlled them.

But these classes could not remould society in their own interests without smashing the old constitution. Like a chicken growing inside an egg, they could and did develop a long way under the old order but eventually they had to smash the shell or be choked.

It took a civil war, a military dictatorship, a 'restoration' and a second revolution to finish the job.

Everybody knows that the Revolution took the form, at the beginning, of a conflict between King Charles and parliament, especially the House of Commons. The Commons had become by the early years of the century a stronghold of the new rich, the growing capitalist class.

'We could buy the Upper House, His Majesty only excepted, thrice over,' boasted an MP in 1628.

The MPs were elected by a very restricted body of property-owning voters who shared their outlook and their aims.

Militia

These men had other sources of power as well as wealth. There was then no local government as we know it today, no police force and no regular army. In the cities the rich merchants ruled through 'corporations' that were generally speaking confined to members of their class.

In the countryside the squires ruled as Justices of the Peace with vastly greater powers than JP's have today. The only permanent armed forces (apart from the navy) were the 'train bands' or militia who were officered for the most part by men of the same classes.

The men who sat in the Commons together with their friends and relatives were, to a large extent, already administering the economically advanced part of the country before the Revolution.

Charles 1

But they were not ruling it. The Stuart kings James and Charles were determined to maintain the old order and to curb the growing power of the new rich.

They were supported by all the most conservative forces in the country, the nobility in its great majority and the smaller landowners of the economically backward parts of the country, the north and the west, where capitalism was still very weak.

In 1629 Charles had told parliament, 'If you do not do your duty, mine would then order me to use those other means which God has put into my hand.' The parliament did not do its 'duty' – that is, it refused to vote the King the large revenues he demanded. It was dismissed after a few weeks.

Charles resorted to his 'other means'. During the eleven years' tyranny that followed, he imprisoned some of the opposition leaders, levied taxes on his own authority and punished those who refused to pay. He compelled rich men to 'loan' him money and secured decisions from the judges (whom he appointed and dismissed at his pleasure) that all these things were allowed by 'the common law and fundamental policy of the kingdom', as Chief Justice Finch put it.

Finch went on to say, 'They are void Acts of parliament [which] bind the King not to command the subjects, their persons and goods and I say their money too, for no Acts of parliament make any difference.'

This blow to their pockets put the merchants and capitalist landowners firmly on the road to revolution.

The crisis came in 1640. Charles had provoked the rebellion in Scotland. He had earlier 'by an Act of revocation annulling grants of property made for more than 80 years' lost the support of the Scottish nobles.

When he attempted to reconstruct the Scottish church on the English model, virtually the entire propertied class revolted and raised an army which made short work of the handful of Royalist supporters in the country.

It may seem strange that a revolution should be triggered off by an attempt to change the management and ritual of a church, but it has to be remembered that the church was then a very important instrument of the government.

The English church was a combined civil service, propaganda ministry and political police. Church attendance was compulsory (non-attenders could be fined) and parsons were required to preach regularly against 'disobedience and wilful rebellion'.

Ritual

Obstinate dissenters were liable to be pilloried, whipped or have their noses split or their ears lopped off. The church defended the existing society in religious terms and so, since practically everybody thought in such terms in those days, the opponents of the old order became religious dissenters.

The Scots church – the kirk – organised on a Presbyterian basis (without bishops, deans and so on) was rather more democratic than the Church of England. James I had said, 'A Scotch Presbytery as well fitteth with monarchy as God with the Devil. No bishop, no king.'

Charles was determined to force bishops on the Scots more effectively than his father had done and to throw in the English ritual for good measure. The Scots, or rather the property owners among them, associated bishops and English church ritual with royal tyranny and they were right.

To force the King to come to terms they sent their army south across the border, defeated a small royalist force at Newburn and occupied Northumberland and Durham.

The English opposition now had its chance. For all his arbitrary taxes and forced 'loans', Charles was dangerously short of money. It was an age of inflation and the traditional sources of royal income were yielding less and less in real terms.

Dismissed

The new rich were more and more evading and even openly resisting the royal demands. To raise an army big enough to deal with the Scots, the King needed their co-operation. He was driven to call a parliament and demand from it the then enormous sum of £840,000.

When it proved unco-operative, he dismissed it after three weeks, but his situation grew even worse and in November 1640 he summoned another, the famous Long Parliament. The first of Lenin's three requirements for a real revolution – that the old ruling class cannot go on in the old way – had been met.

So had the second – that the rising class will not go on in the old way. 'Both their ultimate aims and their immediate programme were in fact revolutionary. The parliamentary leaders, Pym, Elliott, Rouse and the rest, forged the Commons into a revolutionary weapon.'

Charles hoped to appeal to their patriotism. England and Scotland were then separate kingdoms united only by having the same king. There was no love lost between the English and the Scots, they had been fighting each other for centuries. Moreover, the Scots were negotiating with France for an alliance against the English.

The parliamentary leaders taught King Charles a lesson from which we can profit. They would be patriotic when the class they represented was in power. Meanwhile, they would rather see the Scots in London than trust the King with an army.

Appointed

Even when the Catholic Irish broke out in a great rebellion, destroying a good deal of capitalist property and cutting a great many throats, the parliamentary leaders did not falter. They would indeed agree to pay for an army for Ireland – provided that they and they alone appointed its officers and directed its operations.

'By God, not for an hour,' was the King's reply. After an unsuccessful attempt to seize the best known of his opponents by force, he fled north and called on his supporters to join him in arms.

The parliament called a Committee of Public Safety, effectively a war ministry, and rallied its own troops. The civil war had begun.

Part 2:
CIVIL WAR, THEN COMPROMISE

'WE ALL THOUGHT ONE BATTLE WOULD DECIDE,' said one of the 'Roundhead' leaders early in the civil war. In fact the English Revolution was a long drawn-out affair because the capitalist merchants and landowners wanted to win without drawing the mass of the people into the fight.

The parliamentary leaders knew their property would never be safe until they had destroyed the semi-feudal monarchy. They knew too that their heads would be lopped off if the King won.

But they feared the 'small people', the peasants and artisans – there were then few workers of the modern kind – at least as much as they feared the royalists.

Their strategy was to force the King to compromise with them, to become their figurehead in a 'constitutional monarchy', that is to say, one under capitalist control. Accordingly they fought a defensive war and resisted the attempts of the more radical Roundheads to press and fight to a finish.

The truth is that the argument about means (how to win the war) was really about ends (what are we fighting for?). Hardly had the war got under way than this split developed on the Roundhead side.

As usual, at the time, it was put in religious terms. 'This conflict,' writes the Marxist historian Christopher Hill, 'is usually described as one between Presbyterians and Independents...but religion had little to do with it...the real difference was between the win-the-war party and the compromisers.

'It was, in fact, a class split between the big trading bourgeoisie (in other words capitalists) and that section of the aristocracy and big landowners whose interests were bound up with them – Presbyterians – and the progressive smaller gentry, yeomen etc supported by the masses of smaller peasants and artisans – Independents.'

It was a split of a kind that can be seen, again and again

in various revolutions.

On the one hand there is rarely a real revolution until sections of the rising class have actually gained some considerable influence. On the other hand, the sections of the rising class that have got the furthest on the road to power always, invariably, try to compromise with the old order.

To carry through the revolution they have to be pushed aside.

The same sort of thing is true of the working-class movement. The mass of paid officials and leaders that have developed out of the movement always become a brake on the movement.

For several years the Presbyterians controlled the parliamentary armies. There were battles and sieges but always the Presbyterian-controlled parliament avoided pressing the royalists too hard.

Even when the main royal army was shattered at Marston Moor in 1644, the victory was not pressed home and King Charles was given a breathing space to raise fresh forces.

'Without a more speedy, vigorous an effective prosecution of the war', said the Independent leader Oliver Cromwell after Marston Moor, 'we shall make the kingdom weary of us and hate the name of parliament.' The Presbyterian leaders, he said, 'are afraid to conquer.'

The Presbyterian attitude was summed up by a parliamentary general, the Earl of Manchester: 'if we beat the King ninety and nine times, yet he is still King.' To which Cromwell, then Manchester's deputy, replied: 'If this be so, why did we take up arms at first?'

Forced

The conflict between Independents and Presbyterians came to a head when the Independents proposed a 'Self-Denying Ordinance'.

All the senior army commanders were members of the parliament in which the Presbyterians had a large majority.

The bulk of the army, especially the cavalry, were by this time Independents. The Ordinance forbade members of parliament to hold military command, in other words it sacked the Presbyterian generals.

Naturally, the Presbyterians resisted. They were forced to give way, in 1645, under the pressure of their own troops. This was no mere technical change. It meant that parliament had lost supreme power.

From now on power had to be shared with the army, or rather with the army's senior officers who, after the Ordinance, were Independents to a man. The point was driven home when General Cromwell, himself an MP, was declared 'indispensable' by the Army Council and exempted from the Ordinance.

Within three months the reorganised royal army was destroyed at Naseby, the biggest battle of the war, and the King fled north to surrender to the Scots.

What the rich Presbyterians had feared now happened. The 'dirty people of no name', as a royalist writer called them, the small property owners in the ranks of the army, began to take a hand in affairs. They were called Levellers.

Oliver Cromwell

They were, for the most part, young farmers and tradesmen. Their programme, the 'Agreement of the People', called for votes for all property owners, however small, a republic and religious freedom.

The Independent leaders, 'the Grandees' as they were coming to be called, had varying degrees of sympathy with some of these ideas but were themselves substantial property owners. They had no wish to see 'mean and beggarly followers' sharing their power.

Cromwell himself came to believe 'there is no other way to deal with these men but to break them in pieces.'

But the power of the Grandees rested on the army. The Presbyterian-controlled parliament still existed and, in 1646, it bought King Charles from the Scots –

for £400,000, 'the only benefit Scotland ever had from monarchy'.

Alliance

The Presbyterians and the defeated royalists now drew close together and began to intrigue with the King for the sort of compromise the right-wing Presbyterians had always wanted.

The army stood in the way. The parliament tried to disband it, bit by bit, so Cromwell and his associates were

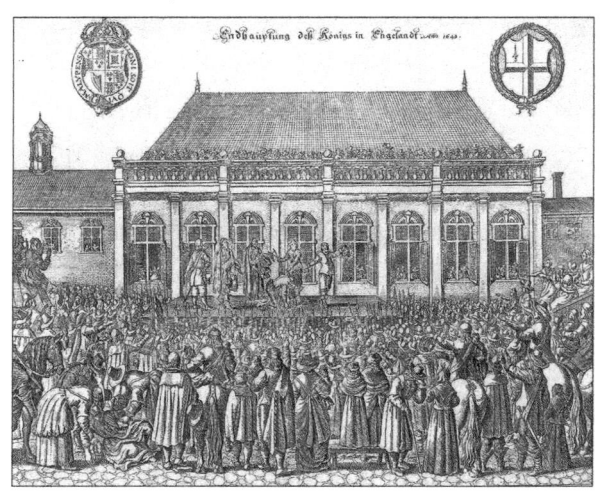

The execution of Charles I, 30 January 1649

forced into alliance with the Levellers. Army and parliament now existed side by side as rival powers in the state.

In 1647 the Independent generals and the Levellers agreed to refuse to disband 'until the liberties of England be secure'. The Army Council was broadened to include elected delegates, called Agitators, from the regiments.

It was not long before the two sides fell out again but in 1648 the King escaped and, supported this time by many of the most conspicuous leaders of the Long Parliament as well as by the Scots, renewed the civil war.

To gain his new support the King had promised to

concede all the original 1640 demands of the Roundheads and had further agreed that Presbyterianism should be the sole religion tolerated in England and Scotland. He reckoned he could deal with his new allies after the revolutionary army had been defeated.

But he was beaten and the Revolution reached its highest point. The Presbyterians were 'purged' from the parliament, leaving an Independent 'Rump'. In January 1649 'that man of blood Charles Stuart' was executed in Whitehall. The House of Lords was abolished and, on 19th May that year, the Republic was proclaimed.

Plunder

Now Cromwell had no further need of the Levellers. The time to break them in pieces had come.

It was done partly by direct force but largely by taking the army to Ireland. Cromwell's conquest of Ireland fastened a foreign rule there that was to last for centuries. It also turned the mass of Leveller supporters into conservative sharers in the plunder.

The defeat of the Levellers meant, in the end, that the Republic could not be maintained. It had against it on the right the great mass of the propertied class, Presbyterians and Royalists, without having a popular effective base of its own.

Cromwell soon quarrelled even with the 'Rump'. This last remnant of the Long Parliament was dispersed by force in 1653 and Cromwell ruled directly through the army, itself purged more than once. The regime collapsed with his death and in 1660 King Charles II was brought to power with the help of the Presbyterians.

Property

It was an unstable agreement and, in 1688, the last Stuart king, James II, was overthrown by what was termed 'The Glorious Revolution'. It was 'glorious' in the eyes of the capitalist class because James II was overthrown by an army of foreign mercenaries commanded by a Dutchman,

William of Orange. No dangerous, levelling, English revolutionary force was needed.

In William of Orange the men of property got the 'constitutional monarch' they wanted. He was a man with no conceivable title to rule but that which parliament gave him, a foreigner unfamiliar with the country and wholly dependent on the new rich capitalist class.

With the revolution of 1688 they came to rule the country in their own interests. Thay have been doing so ever since. They will go on doing so until the working class makes its own revolution.

Part 3:
REVOLT BY 'COLONIALS' THAT LAUNCHED THE USA

'WE HOLD THESE TRUTHS TO BE SELF-EVIDENT, that all men are created equal, that they are endowed by their creator with certain inalienable rights, that among these are life, liberty, and the pursuit of happiness... That whenever any form of government becomes destructive to these ends it is the right of the people to alter or abolish it... That these united colonies are, and of right ought to be, Free and Independent states, and that all political connection between them and the state of Great Britain is, and ought to be, totally dissolved.'

The men who put their names to this, the American Declaration of Independence on the fourth of July 1776, were the leaders of the first successful colonial revolution.

From the point of view of the British ruling class and – what is much the same thing – in the eyes of the law, they were traitors. 'We must all hang together,' said one of them, 'or we will all hang separately' and that was literally true.

Treason, of course, is a political crime but a rather special one because, as the old saying has it, 'Treason never prospers; for if it doth it is no longer treason.' The traitors of 1776 were successful. They became the founding fathers of the United States of America.

They were, for the most part, rich men. Like the leaders of the English Revolution in the previous century, they became revolutionaries to protect and increase their wealth. They believed, with good reason, that it was threatened by continued British rule.

An American historian wrote of the delegates to the first Continental Congress: 'They were the American aristocracy; the merchants, the lawyers and the great planters of the South.'

Advocates

This was clear enough to the British rulers of colonial America. 'The plan of the people of property,' wrote the British General Gage, 'has been to raise the lower classes... without the influence and instigation of these [the wealthy] the inferior people would have been very quiet.'

And an English Tory drew the attention to a very peculiar fact about the American advocates of the 'Rights of Man'. 'Why is it,' he asked, 'that the loudest yelps for liberty come from the drivers of slaves?'

It was partly true. George Washington was a slave-owner. So was Patrick Henry, the radical who proclaimed, 'Give me Liberty or give me Death.'

The developing capitalist class in America, for that was what the revolutionary leaders represented was not oppressed by a semi-feudal monarchy. That had been destroyed in Britain in the seventeenth century revolutions.

It was oppressed by the 'colonial system' operated in the interests of British capitalists. The colonies were run as sources of raw materials for British industry and markets for British manufacturers' surplus.

The colonists were forbidden to manufacture ironware of any kind. That was reserved for British ironmasters. The Americans could make iron, but only for export to Britain.

They were forbidden to manufacture woollen goods and even hats and caps. No competition with the most important English textile industry was allowed. The Americans must buy British.

The British Board of Trade spelt out its policy in a statement some twenty years before the revolution. 'Encouraging manufactures which in any way interfere with the manufactures of this Kingdom, has always been thought improper, and has ever been discouraged.'

Equally important was the British control of trade. The most important colonial exports, tobacco, cotton, rice, indigo, iron, timber and, after 1776, even fish and flour, could be legally sent only to Britain.

British merchants naturally took advantage of their monopoly position. And imports from countries other than Britain were either forbidden or subject to such heavy taxes that they could not compete with British goods. The Americans had to pay the extra prices.

In these circumstances smuggling became a major American industry. For example, sugar and molasses (for making rum) could be bought in the French West Indian islands for up to 40 per cent below the British prices.

Respectable

Fortunes were made by smuggling in illegal French molasses and sugar in exchange for the equally illegal export of American goods. Some idea of the scale of this criminal activity can be seen from the estimate that in 1763 some 15,000 hogsheads of molasses were imported into Massachusetts and only 500 of them paid the tax.

The men who operated this huge defiance of the law were not petty criminals. They were highly respectable citizens, great merchants and ship owners, like John Hancock of Boston, who signed the Declaration of Independence in extra-large letters so that, as he said, the King of England would read his name without using spectacles.

The revolutionary crisis was sparked off, as commonly happens, by the government. In 1763, at the end of the seven years' war with France, the British government permanently took over French Canada, thus freeing the colonies of the threat of the French and their Indian allies and so making British rule less acceptable.

It then went on to tighten its control over American trade. It reinforced its naval patrols against smugglers.

Lexington 19 April 1775: American revolution began when 'rebels' opened fire and scattered the redcoats

More troops were sent to America to enforce 'law and order' of the British capitalist variety and new laws were introduced to tax the American colonists so that they might pay for the privilege of being oppressed.

'No taxation without representation' became the popular slogan. But in fact the more radical colonial leaders did not want representation in the British parliament. There they would be a permanent minority.

They wanted independence.

One thing that helped them win the support of large numbers of poorer Americans was the 'Proclamation' by which the British government forbade the colonists to move across the Allegheny mountains into what is now the Middle West. Poor men were prevented from getting land of their own.

The radicals developed political organisations, the Sons of Liberty and the Committees of Correspondence. They organised demonstrations and riots, like the Boston Tea Party, to destroy British goods.

They clashed with British troops. And gradually they gained the support of a large active minority of the colonists.

It was on 19 April 1775, at the little town of Lexington near Boston, that in the words of the American poet, Emerson, 'the embattled farmers stood and fired the shots heard round the world'.

The British regulars were beaten at Lexington. Not many of them it is true, for the famous battle was a very small affair. But the moral effect was tremendous. From then on all compromise was impossible.

The men who fought at Lexington were not merchant princes or great planters. They were poor men. And throughout the long hard struggle until the decisive defeat of the British at Yorktown, Virginia, in 1781 'the men of the revolutionary army, for the greater part, were plain people, the small farmers, the frontiersmen, in short the poorer classes.'

They fought because they believed they were fighting for a new world. And basically, in spite of slavery in the South, in spite of the fact that the revolution was 'a rich man's war but a poor man's fight,' they were right.

Advance

It was a rich man's war, but it was not only a rich man's war. The men who came to rule the new American republic were not 'plain people', they were the American capitalist class. But the republic was undoubtedly an advance, politically and economically, even for the majority of poor Americans.

The American Revolution was a capitalist revolution – a bourgeois revolution in Marxist language – but it was a capitalist revolution at a time when capitalism was still a progressive system, the best then possible.

It was a step forward in America. And not only in America.

The ideas of the Declaration of Independence, of the Rights of Man, soon came back to a Europe that was still, Britain and a few small countries apart, semi-feudal and they came back with the prestige of a successful revolution behind them.

They helped to ignite the great French Revolution.

Part 4:
'TERRIBLE ONES' TAKE UP ARMS

ONE EVENING IN THE SUMMER OF 1789 King Louis XVI of France returned to his palace at Versailles after a day's hunting. He wrote in his diary '14 July, nothing'. No other ruler ever made a bigger mistake.

That morning some twenty miles away in Paris a large crowd had broken into the barracks at the Hotel des Invalides and carried off the 30,000 muskets stored there. Then, reinforced by mutinous soldiers of the royal army, they stormed the great fortress of the Bastille. The head of the royal governor, the Marquis de Launey, was paraded round the streets on a pike.

'The capture of the Bastille seemed miraculous to an age

accustomed to scoff at miracles. That a massive medieval castle strengthened with artillery and a garrison should have surrendered, after a few hours fighting, to a civilian crowd stiffened by a few soldiers might well puzzle a professional mind,' wrote the historian J.M. Thompson.

'The day was, in fact, won by the moral force of the people. It was sympathy with the people which forced the garrison to surrender.'

The victory was not bloodless. At least nintey-eight of the attackers were killed together with six of the defenders. But basically Thompson is right.

For King Louis was not short of troops. He had 270,000 regulars and had concentrated twenty regiments in and around Paris. A good proportion of these were foreign mercenaries, mostly German and Swiss, who the royal commanders regarded as especially reliable for use against the people.

This massive force proved useless. The French guards mutinied, so did sections of the artillery. All the soldiers were affected by the tremendous enthusiasm and hopes of the people of Paris for 'Liberty, Equality, Fraternity'.

The royal commander de Broglie, evacuated Paris on the 15th. He could not, he told the King, rely on his men. 'Even the foreign regiments are of doubtful loyalty.' The old regime was finished. It was a turning point in world history.

Bread

The Paris Revolution of 14 July 1789 did not, of course, come out of the blue, nor was it unorganised. It came after months of rioting in the cities. After the spring of 1789 there was hardly a town which had not seen one or more of these incidents or rebellions and they were doubly frequent in July.

The immediate cause was economic. The harvest of 1788 was bad and bread, the staple diet of the mass of the French people, was both scarce and dear. Speaking of the Paris workmen the French historian George Lefebvre wrote: 'For him to live, it was estimated that bread should cost no more than two sous a pound. In the first half of July the price was twice this figure.'

But there had been scarcity, indeed famine, before. Bread riots were nothing new. What was new was the fact that this time the riots coincided with a profound political crisis. The royal government could not go on in the old way. The developing capitalist class would not go on in the old way.

Of the twenty-three million Frenchmen and women on the eve of the great revolution, about 400,000 were

The National Assembly meets on a tennis court to defy the King

nobles. There were also about 100,000 clergy, including monks and so on. These were the first two 'estates', the legally privileged. The other 22.5 million made up the Third Estate.

The nobles were at the top of the social heap. They had a monopoly of commissions in the army and navy. Every government minister but one was a noble in 1789.

They monopolised the higher offices of the church. Every bishop was a noble and the church they controlled 'enjoyed immense wealth, privileges and authority; the value of its properties represented something between two-fifths and a half of the landed wealth in every province and it was exempt from all taxation.'

All nobles were exempt from the most important kind of tax and, in practice, virtually all direct taxation. Some nobles were immensely wealthy, some relatively poor. All got their incomes, apart from salaries from positions in church and state, from the feudal dues extorted from the peasants.

Destitution

The peasants, by far the biggest group of the population, were at the bottom of the social heap. Most of them were legally free although one million were still serfs. Their economic position varied from ordinary poverty to absolute destitution.

Society rested on the backs of the peasants. They paid rent in money or goods to the feudal landowner. They paid him to inherit their holding, they paid him for the privilege of transferring it by exchange.

They were compelled to use the lord's mill, winepress and bakery at his charges or to pay for exemption. In the event of a dispute the matter was settled in the lord's own private court.

The peasants were compelled to pay the tithe, the tax to the church, usually in produce. They were subject to forced labour without pay for road repairs and various other 'public works'.

On top of all this they were mercilessly squeezed by the state. Since the privileged orders paid no taxes or very light ones the whole burden fell on the Third Estate, but above all on the peasants. The peasant was almost alone in paying the 'taille' – the main direct tax. From this came most of the proceeds of the poll tax.

The royal demands had risen steadily. The increase in direct taxes in the reign of Louis XVI alone had been estimated at 28 per cent.

The average French peasant was paying out in feudal dues, tithes and taxes the greater part of his meagre income. When the harvest failed in 1788 his position became desperate. The Revolution gained an immense reserve force.

'Who would dare to deny that the Third Estate has within itself all that is necessary to constitute a nation? Take away the privileged orders, and the nation is not smaller, but greater. This privileged class is assuredly foreign to the nation by its uselessness.'

Joseph Sieyès wrote this declaration of war upon nobility in his famous pamphlet 'What is the Third Estate?' He made himself spokesman for the merchants and financiers, lawyers and the small but growing group of industrial capitalists – the bourgeoisie as they were called in French.

They were similar in many ways to the English Presbyterians of the previous century but, as times had changed, they no longer put their political ideas in religious terms. They spoke the language of the American revolutionaries and talked of the Rights of Man.

'For centuries the bourgeois, envious of the aristocracy, had aimed only at thrusting into its ranks.' There was in fact a considerable number of nobles of recent bourgeois origin but it was becoming harder to make the transition. With increasing wealth the numbers and ambitions of the bourgeois continued to mount, and the aristocracy, losing ground to the new rich, was closing its ranks to the new interlopers.

More and more the French bourgeois class looked to the examples of England and America and accepted revolutionary ideas. The crisis came in 1789 for the same reason that it came in England in 1640. The royal government was bankrupt. The privileged classes, and many of the richer merchants, were either exempt from taxation or evaded it and the peasants and the town poor could be squeezed no further.

It was to remedy the financial crisis that King Louis agreed to call representatives of the three estates, the States-General, to meet for the first time since 1614. They had no sooner met in May 1789 than they fell out.

'By heads'

The old rule was that the States-General voted 'by orders', that is each estate met and voted separately and a majority of estates was needed for any proposal. The 621 representatives of the Third Estate, practically all of them bourgeois, were thus put in a permanent minority by the 593 representatives of the first two orders. They wanted voting 'by heads' so that their greater numbers could give them a permanent majority.

This dispute could not be resolved and on 17 June the Third Estate proclaimed itself, quite illegally, as the National Assembly, the representatives of the whole French people, and invited members of other estates to join them as individuals.

On 20 June they were excluded from their meeting hall, and, gathering in an indoor tennis court, resolved 'that all members of this Assembly shall at once take a solemn oath never to separate' until a constitution had been agreed to.

This act of defiance of the King led him to resort to force. He concentrated his troops and prepared to disperse the Assembly but first he had to make sure of Paris.

The rising of 14 July, which was stirred up by radical bourgeois agitators, put paid to that. The bourgeois class seemed to have gained an easy victory.

But the men who stormed the Bastille were not, in the great majority, bourgeois. They were workmen and small masters. Having come onto the political stage 'the terrible people of Paris' were not going to disappear so easily.

And the peasants were now on the move. Far from ending on 14 July, theRevolution had only just begun.

Part 5:
EQUALITY – BUT ONLY FOR THE FEW

'Feudalism has been totally abolished.' So the French National Assembly proclaimed after its session of 4 August 1789. That night some 30 decrees abolished serfdom, feudal rents, forced labour, the private courts of the lords, the personal and tax privileges of nobles and clergy and a host of other feudal institutions.

The Assembly further resolved that a medal should be struck to commemorate this great occasion, 'the restoration of French liberty'.

Not everyone was impressed. 'It is by the light from the flames of their burning chateaux,' wrote the left-wing Jacobin Jean-Paul Marat, 'that they magnanimously renounce the privilege of holding in chains men who have already recovered their freedom by force.'

Marat was right. There had been peasant risings even before 14 July and after the fall of the Bastille a great torrent of peasant revolt swept France.

Peasants broke into the great country houses of the nobles and burnt the feudal title deeds that listed the payments required of them. If they were resisted they sometimes burnt the chateaux for good measure.

They refused to pay either feudal dues or the 'compensation' to the feudal lords that the Assembly tried to insist on. For the peasants, feudalism had been 'totally abolished' by their own efforts, no matter what the Assembly might say.

Deprived
'Men are born, and always continue, free and equal in respect of their rights...and these rights are Liberty, Property, Security and Resistance to Oppression.' These opening words of the Declaration of the Rights of Man, issued by the National Assembly in August, were a 'violent and daring assertion of principles destructive of the constituted authorities of all Europe.' For the very essence

of feudal law and feudal society was that men are not born equal, that they do not have equal rights.

Yet the declaration also had its conservative side. Article 17 spelt it out. 'The right to property being inviolable and sacred, no one ought to be deprived of it, except in case of evident public necessity, legally ascertained, and on condition of a just indemnity paid in advance.'

This was, after all, a capitalist revolution. Those burning chateaux haunted the middle-class members of the Assembly.

From now on they were conservatives, the majority (called Feuillants) more afraid of the masses than of the feudal reaction. This was shown very clearly in the constitution they adopted. The King was to remain and was to be effective head of the government, choosing his own ministers like an American president.

He was to have no power to make or alter laws – that was reserved for a Legislative Assembly – but he was given the power to veto acts of the Assembly for four years. The Assembly was to be elected by a tiny minority, some 43,000 electors, qualifying by ownership of substantial wealth.

The two-sided nature of the National Assembly, revolutionary with respect to feudalism, reactionary with respect to peasants and town workers, is seen in all its acts. On the one hand it abolished legal torture, the normal means of securing a confession of crime under the old regime (nobles, of course, were exempt) together with barbarous methods of capital punishment, breaking on the wheel, burning and so on.

Decapitation, before 1789 an aristocratic privilege, was now open to all! On the other hand it passed a 'Law of Associations' which absolutely forbade trade union activity of any kind.

It takes two sides to compromise. King Louis refused to accept the Rights of Man or the Decrees of 4 August, 'I will never consent,' he wrote, 'to the spoilation of my clergy or my nobility.' Like Charles I before him, he was determined to restore the old order and looked to the forces of feudal reaction, at home and abroad, to come to his aid. The deadlock was broken, not by the assembly, but by the working people of Paris.

These 'sans-culottes', so-called because they wore workmen's trousers instead of the knee breeches then favoured by the respectable classes, were small masters, independent craftsmen or wage earners in small shops. They were the ones who had stormed the Bastille and they now drove the Revolution forward.

In July a middle-class National Guard had been established under the command of the Feuillant leader,

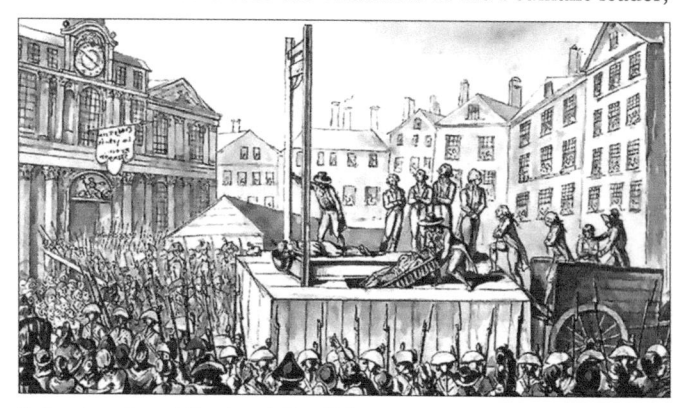

The 'terror': counter-revolutionaries go to the guillotine

the Marquis de Lafayette. Its members had to be wealthy enough to pay for their own uniforms, arms and equipment.

They, it was hoped, would keep the sans-culottes in order now that the army was unusable. It failed. In October 1789 'the mob', as reactionary historians call the common people, swept the National Guard along with it, marched to Versailles, disarmed the King's bodyguard and brought him back to Paris, effectively a prisoner. The Assembly followed.

Louis was now compelled to swallow his 'never' and put his name to the Declaration and the decrees. He was playing for time. The counter-revolution was getting organised. Over the border in western Germany thousands of French nobles, the emigres, were raising troops.

Louis and his supporters were not the only ones who wanted war. In June 1791 Louis escaped from Paris and fled towards the émigré camps. He was caught at Varennes and brought back under guard.

The flight to Varennes created an openly republican party in the assembly but its right wing, the Girondins, were every bit as property-conscious and afraid of the sans-culottes as the Feuillants. By the end of the year Louis had appointed Girondin ministers and they saw a war as a means of halting further revolutionary developments.

Only the left wing of the republicans, the Jacobins, opposed the war policy. 'People do not like missionaries with bayonets,' said Maximilian Robespierre, the Jacobin leader, replying to the argument that people everywhere would rise against their leaders if the French invaded their countries.

Robespierre saw clearly that the war party was a coalition of out and out counter-revolutionaries who hoped for the defeat of France together with Girondist conservatives who hoped to spill the blood of the sans-culottes on foreign battlefields. He saw too, that a united foreign intervention was by no means inevitable.

The rulers of the great semi-feudal powers, Austria, Prussia, Russia, detested the Revolution but they also feared and distrusted each other. The rulers of capitalist Britain, traditional rivals of France, half feared and half welcomed the Revolution which, they hoped, would weaken their enemy.

But the Girondins and the King got their way. On 20 April 1792 Louis declared war on Austria, starting a conflict that was to last for more than twenty years and involve every power in Europe.

On the top of this, armed counter-revolution broke out inside France itself, in the south and the west. The Revolution was in deadly peril.

It was saved again by the people of Paris. On 10 August

the sans-culottes, led by Jacobins, seized the town hall and established the Commune, a more or less democratic town government. They went on to storm the royal palace and seize the King. The National Guard was 'democratised' and the Commune became the effective ruling power.

It forced the Assembly to dissolve itself and order the election of a National Convention by universal manhood suffrage. Early in September some 1,200 royalists were tried for treason and guillotined. The Prussian army was now at Verdun, barely 200 miles from Paris. Volunteers, overwhelmingly sans-culottes, were rushed to the front supported by contingents from Marseilles and Brest.

The defeat of the Prussians at Valmy on 20 September saved Paris but the situation was still desperate. Spain, Holland and Britain soon declared war.

The National Convention, which had a Girondist majority, was forced to recognise the Commune and put effective power in the hands of a wholly Jacobin Committee of Public Safety. King Louis was executed and the French Republic proclaimed.

The internal counter-revolution gained control of a considerable part of France and the hastily assembled revolutionary armies on the frontiers suffered a series of defeats.

This was the background to the reign of terror by which Robespierre, Carnot and the other members of the Committee of Public Safety saved the Revolution. It was a savage enough regime. The guillotine was in constant requisition.

But it was the essential instrument to defeat an immensely powerful armed counter-revolution. By 1794 the back of the internal resistance had been broken.

The Jacobin dictatorship was overthrown as soon as the immediate threat had passed (July 1794, 9 Thermidor on the new revolutionary calendar). The sans-culottes, its essential support, were in the armies or exhausted. A conservative Directory took over, to be overthrown in 1799 by General Bonaparte.

But the essential gains of the Revolution remained. The German poet Goethe, who had been with the Prussian army at Valmy, had said after the battle: 'From this place and from this day forth commences a new era in the history of the world.' That will stand as the best epitaph of the revolution itself.

Part 6:
TURNING POINT: 1848 – THE WORKERS COME ONTO THE STAGE

'FROM MARCH TO JUNE 1848 HYMNS TO LIBERTY and fraternity had rebounded from Paris to Poznan and Bucharest, from Holstein to Sicily. Two great states alone escaped the contagion; industrial England, capitalist and liberal, and agricultural Russia, feudal and autocratic.'

The revolutions of 1848 were the most widespread ever until 1917-19. 1848 saw the last large-scale attempts at middle-class revolution in Europe. It saw too, the first large-scale intervention of a political working-class movement with aims of its own.

The two facts are, of course, connected. In the field of ideas, 1848 saw European nationalism turn from a progressive force into a partly reactionary one, and socialism become, for the first time, a significant political movement.

The *Communist Manifesto* appeared in 1848 and some of the most important political writings of Marx and Engels are based on their experiences in 'the year of revolutions'.

Why in 1848? The great French Revolution of 1789-94

had completely destroyed the remains of feudalism in France and led to 23 years of war in which feudal Europe had been shaken to its foundations.

Shaken but not destroyed. In 1814-15 the final defeat of France by an all-European coalition appeared 'to set the seal on the triumph of reaction'.

The Russian, Austrian and Prussian empires established a 'Holy Alliance' which, guided by 'the principle of Christianity', was to uphold by force 'legitimacy', otherwise known as 'Divine Right of Kings', all over Europe.

In fact the restoration of the old order was only partial.

Back to 'Liberty, Equality and Brotherhood' – a Paris meeting in 1848

In France itself the Bourbon kings, of whom it was said had 'learned nothing and forgotten nothing', were restored. But the peasants kept the land and the capitalist legal system remained in force.

Feudalism was not and could not be restored. And in the Netherlands, western Germany, Switzerland and a good part of Italy, all occupied by the French during the wars, the same thing was true.

Savage
Absolute monarchs ruled (except in Switzerland) over basically capitalist societies. It was a situation as unstable as that in England between the restoration of the Stuart Kings in 1660 and the Revolution of 1688.

East of the Elbe and the Alps it was a very different matter. Serfdom remained common. The privileges of the nobility flourished.

The middle classes, let alone the peasants and workers, were excluded from all power. There was no equality before the law. Jews were confined to their ghettoes and political or even religious dissent was savagely repressed. The middle ages were still alive.

One feature of the restored 'old order' needs special mention. The 'Divine Right of Kings' to rule where their ancestors were supposed to have ruled took no account of language or national feeling.

Germany was divided into thirty-nine states, most of them very small, each with its absolute ruler. Italy was similarly carved up.

The Austrian Emperor included Germans, Hungarians, Italians, Czechs, Poles, Croats, Slovaks, Slovenes, Ukrainians and Rumanians among his subjects. The official language of the Empire was Latin and the fact that it was not understood by ordinary people anywhere was not regarded as a disadvantage. Ordinary people had no business to concern themselves with matters of government.

The ideals of the French Revolution were everywhere driven underground but they were not killed. The rights of man, democracy and nationalism were preached by secret revolutionary societies. Already in 1820-21 the Holy Alliance had been compelled to intervene to put down revolutionary movements in Italy and Spain.

Between 1821 and 1827 the Greek people established their independence against their 'legitimate' ruler, the Turkish Sultan. In 1830 the Belgians successfully overthrew the rule of the King of Holland which had been imposed on them in 1815.

There was an unsuccessful Polish rising against the Tsar in the same year and in 1847 the Swiss middle-class radicals overthrew the reactionary constitution of 1815 and defeated the reactionaries in the civil war that followed.

In 1848 the dam burst. The French Revolution of February 1848 led to revolution, generally successful at first, over the greater part of Europe.

The last 'legitimate' Bourbon King of France had already been driven out 18 years earlier and replaced by the 'July monarchy' of King Louis-Philippe. But, as Marx wrote, 'Under Louis-Philippe it was not the French bourgeoisie [capitalists] as a whole which ruled but only one fraction of it...the so-called financial aristocracy...the interests of the industrial bourgeoisie were inevitably in permanent peril and at a permanent disadvantage under this system.'

Legal, 'constitutional' opposition was ineffective and became more and more difficult as the regime sensed the revolutionary groundswell. Underground societies, some purely middle class and republican, some already partly working class and socialist, planned armed risings.

There were unsuccessful attempts in Paris in 1832 and 1839 and at Lyons in 1834. By February 1848 the different strands of opposition, legal and illegal, from wealthy capitalists to pioneer socialist leaders, had come together in the same agitation for an end to the repression and a 'democratic' government.

Their efforts were reinforced, as in 1789, by an economic crisis but this time it was a capitalist crisis. A slump had developed in 1847.

Troops

After clashes and shootings in central Paris, barricades were thrown up across the narrow streets of the working-class east end, more than 1,500 of them, manned by working men and women. The middle-class National Guard would not move against them. The regular troops were influenced by the National Guard and refused to obey their officers.

Louis-Philippe fled to England and a provisional republican government hastily proclaimed the Second Republic. Liberty, Equality and Fraternity were to be restored, or so it was promised.

This was to be the last time that middle-class and working-class revolutionaries were to fight on the same side. Much earlier, in the English and American revolutions and in the great French Revolution, fear of the 'lower orders' had played a big part in the policies of the middle-class leaders. From now on it was to be the main consideration.

Capitalism was developing, a modern working class was coming into existence, a force potentially much greater than the sans-culottes of fifty odd years earlier.

The republicans were forced to proclaim 'The Government of the French Republic binds itself to guarantee the livelihood of the workers by providing work, it will guarantee work for all citizens. It recognises that workers may organise in order to enjoy the fruits of their labour.'

During the next four months the middle-class republicans organised to smash the workers who had forced this concession out of them. In June the republican general Cavaignac was able to use a reconstituted 'republican' army to bloodily suppress the resistance of the socialist-led workers of Paris, inflicting, according to the official underestimate, at least 10,000 casualties.

Power

This bloodletting paved the way for the end of the Second Republic and the installation of a new Bonapartist dictatorship under Napoleon's nephew in 1852.

Outside France the King of Prussia and the Emperor of Austria saw their power broken by successful risings in Berlin and Vienna. The Pope was driven out of Rome and a Roman Republic proclaimed.

The Hungarians and Czechs threw off Austrian rule. All over Germany and Italy middle-class revolutionaries appeared to be in control and from Scandinavia to the Balkans rulers hastened to offer constitutions and concessions.

But, as in France, middle-class fear of workers and peasants was stronger than the will to carry through the capitalist revolution. Engels wrote of the 'National Assembly of the German People', the Frankfurt talking shop as he contemptuously called it, 'This Assembly of old women was, from the first day, more frightened of the least popular movement than of all the reactionary plots of all the German governments put together.' So it was everywhere.

The reactionaries and the old rulers were able to play on this fear and they were also able to exploit the newly awakened national feelings; setting Czechs against Germans, Croats against Hungarians, Germans against Poles. And with the aid of the Tsar's armies they partly, but only partly, recovered their power.

1848 was the great turning point. From now on the middle classes became more and more conservative. They could no longer produce a Cromwell, a Washington or a Robespierre.

The whole cause of progress, from this time forward, comes to depend on the movement of which we are part – the revolutionary socialist movement based on the working class.

Part 7:
1871: THE FIRST WORKERS' STATE

ON 2 SEPTEMBER 1870 THE FRENCH EMPEROR, Louis Napoleon Bonaparte, surrendered himself and 104,000 of his soldiers to the King of Prussia at Sedan near the Luxemburg frontier. It was the end for the French Second Empire. Two days later a new republic was proclaimed in Paris.

The war between France and Prussia had been provoked by Louis Napoleon's government on a frivolous pretext, 'on a mere point of etiquette', said an English paper. But the underlying causes ran deeper.

Louis Napoleon had been elected president of the Second Republic at the end of 1848. He posed as the champion of the peasant and the working man, as opposed to the middle-class republicans who had organised the slaughter of Paris workers in June 1848. At the same time he promised 'law and order'.

In 1852, with the support of the army and the police, he declared the republic abolished and proclaimed himself Emperor. The workers, savagely resentful of the June massacre, did not lift a finger to defend the middle-class republic. From then on flag-waving and drum-beating about the 'glories' of France under the first Napoleon and military adventures abroad became more and more the mainstay of the regime.

'The Second Empire,' wrote Frederick Engels,' was the appeal to French chauvinism... Hence the necessity for occasional wars and extensions of frontiers.'

Desperate Gamble

Louis Napoleon engaged in wars in Russia (the Crimean War), Italy, Africa, China (along with the British in 1860) and Mexico where he attempted to establish a puppet 'Emperor'. In 1870, in a desperate gamble to ward off growing opposition in France, he undertook his last adventure – war with Bismarck's Prussia, since 1866 the strongest power in Germany.

The gamble ended at Sedan. A republican 'Government of National Defence' was formed to 'resist the Prussian invaders'. Soon the Prussian army arrived outside Paris.

The new government organised 'a mock defence of Paris... General Trochu, its agent, flung away his men in useless sorties, mismanaged and disorganised the National Guard... That this policy was deliberate was shown by later discoveries of correspondence.'

In 1792-93 the revolutionary forces had beaten and driven out the invading armies of Prussia, Austria, Britain and Spain, as well as crushing a massive domestic counter-revolution. New armies had been built with former NCOs and civilians as commanders.

Revolutionary 'Commissaires' were put alongside the generals, old and new, and by a liberal use of the guillotine and the firing squad, large numbers of treacherous officers had been eliminated. The entire resources of the country were mobilised in defence of the republic.

That was eighty years earlier and in those eighty years the middle classes had become eighty times more conservative. There was to be no revolutionary mobilisation this time. Better the Prussians than the red!

The French armies, which still controlled most of the country, were led by Bonapartists, by royalists, by reactionaries who feared the consequences of a victory won by popular resistance more than they feared defeat.

Conflict

'Paris,' wrote Karl Marx, 'was not to be defended without arming its working class, organising them into an effective force, and training their ranks by the war itself. But Paris armed was the Revolution armed. A victory of Paris over the Prussian aggressor would have been a victory of the French workman over the French capitalist and his State parasites.

'In this conflict between national duty and class interest, the Government of National Defence did not hesitate for one moment to turn into a Government of National Defection.'

The siege of Paris lasted from mid-September to near the end of January 1871, '135 days of the worst winter within living memory, a winter of Siberian cold, with famine and epidemics.'

No serious attempt was made to organise forces for the relief of the city because, as Marx had noted, the backbone of the defence had come to be the armed workers organised in the battalions of the originally middle-class National Guard.

The 'ultra-patriotic' republican government, while proclaiming in public 'we will not cede an inch of our territory, not a stone of our fortresses', was concerned, before anything else, to arrange for the surrender of the capital city and a peace at almost any price with the King of Prussia.

It succeeded. On 27 January an armistice was signed which provided for the surrender of Paris. In March a peace treaty was agreed, a treaty that involved the ceding to Prussia of two provinces that had been French since the seventeenth century.

But the treacherous republican government, now established at the old royalist capital, Versailles, was not able to arrange for the immediate disarming of the Paris National Guard.

'Armed Paris,' in Marx's words, 'was the only serious obstacle in the way of the counter-revolutionary conspiracy.' In February the National Guard had reorganised itself on the basis of elected officers, subject to recall, and established a central committee with a socialist majority. The Bonapartist officers fled or were dismissed.

In March the Versailles government sent troops into Paris to seize the 400 pieces of artillery in the hands of the Guard. The attempt failed and the central committee took full control of the city. It ordered immediate elections for a democratic commune.

It took over on 28 March. Marx's classic description of it can hardly be improved.

'The Commune was formed of the municipal councillors, chosen by universal suffrage in the various wards... responsible and revocable at short terms. The majority of its members were naturally working men...

'The Commune was to be a working, not a parliamentary body, executive and legislative at the same time...the police was at once stripped of its political attributes and turned into the responsible and at all times revocable

Barricade, across rue Voltaire, Paris 1871

agent of the Commune. So were the officials of all other branches of the administration.

'From the members of the Commune downwards, the public service had to be done at workmen's wages... Having got rid of the standing army and the police, the physical force elements of the old government...the priests were sent back to the recesses of private life...

'Like the rest of public servants, magistrates and judges were to be elective, responsible and revocable.'

This revolutionary, democratic regime which, as

Engels said, 'must necessarily have led in the end to communism,' was, however, isolated in Paris. A member of the Commune, Milliere, shrewdly noted:

'In Paris and some other great towns the working class is sufficiently prepared to attempt it [the revolution] successfully; but in most small towns and particularly in the villages it is as yet incapable of it. Therein lies the great danger to the revolution that has begun in Paris.'

France in 1871 was still predominantly a peasant and rural country and the peasants, unlike those of Russia in 1917, were predominantly conservative since they enjoyed the fruits of the great Revolution of 1789.

There were riots or attempted risings in support of the Commune at Marseilles, Lyons, St. Etienne, Limoges and a few other places. But there was no nationwide revolutionary movement. The Versailles government kept control, helped by the Prussians, who returned tens of thousands of French prisoners to help the counter-revolution.

On 2 April the Versailles army began its assault on Paris. Until the end of May the National Guard maintained a heroic resistance, 'the Parisian workers throughout the struggle did the impossible.'

In the end, weight of numbers and superior equipment enabled the counter-revolutionary troops to break in. A large part of central Paris was destroyed in the fighting and after the last pockets of resistance had been destroyed the forces of 'law and order' exacted a most bloody revenge.

There were wholesale shootings of men, women and children; 'only 14,000' according to the Bonapartist General McMahon, 30,000 according to left-wing writers.

These were followed by 'legal' executions (i.e. after trial) and massive deportations of workers to tropical colonies. By these means the 'democratic' Third Republic, which lasted until 1940, was established.

For Marx the Commune marked 'a new point of departure of world-wide importance,' the first workers' state and the model for those to come.

Twenty years later Engels summed it up: 'do you want to know what the dictatorship of the proletariat looks like? Look at the Paris Commune. That was the dictatorship of the proletariat.'

Part 8:
DRESS REHEARSAL FOR OCTOBER

'THE FURTHER EAST ONE GOES IN EUROPE, the weaker, meaner and more cowardly becomes the capitalist class, and the greater the cultural and political tasks which fall to the lot of the working class. On its strong shoulders the Russian working class must and will carry the work of conquering political liberty.

'This is an essential step, but only the first step, to the realisation of the great historic mission of the working class, to the foundation of a social order in which there will be no place for the exploitation of man by man.'

This statement appeared in the Manifesto issued by the first illegal national Marxist conference in 1898 and it was right. What these pioneer Russian Marxists were saying was: The backward, half medieval Russian Empire needs a capitalist revolution like that of England in the seventeenth century or France in the eighteenth but the Russian capitalist class is incapable of leading it. The workers must do the job.

It was a matter of timing. Russian capitalism was a very late developer. It did not exist in 1848 when the European capitalist classes took their decisive turn to conservatism for fear of the growing working classes.

There was then no modern industry and no modern working class in Russia. Most of the Russian people, the peasants, were still serfs.

In the last years of the last century and the first years of the present one, a great change came. Industry developed in Russia, fuelled by foreign loans and foreign technicians.

With industry came new classes: a capitalist class and a modern working class. By 1914 there were about five million workers in Russia out of a population of around 160 million.

The despotic rule of the Tsar rested on the old society of peasants exploited by nobles and it maintained the laws and customs of the old order. It was an obstacle to rapid capitalist development just as the absolute monarch had been in England and France.

But the Russian capitalists saw that socialist ideas had taken root among workers in some of the more advanced countries and were spreading even in backward Russia. Revolution was now too risky for them. Better the Tsar than the dangers of a revolution that might go beyond the stage of capitalism.

So it came about that the underground Russian socialist organisations had to think in terms of combining a struggle for a 'Rights of Man' type of revolution with preparation for a socialist revolution. The splits and conflicts among them centred around how this was to be done. But the dispute about means really concealed a difference about ends. This would become clear in 1917.

The 'dress rehearsal', as Lenin called it, came in 1905. The previous year the Tsar had plunged his empire into war with Japan.

It was an imperialist war on both sides, a war for plunder, for the control of North China and Korea. The Russians were beaten, a direct result of the corruption and backwardness of Tsardom.

It was the first time for more than a century that an Asiatic power had beaten a European one and this had a profound effect on the colonial world. The white man was not invincible after all. Nationalist movements in the 'Third World' countries got a great impetus. But the biggest immediate effect was in Russia itself.

'The attitude of the masses towards the war in far-off Manchuria was at first one of indifference,' wrote the Bolshevik historian Pokrovsky. 'It was only after repeated mobilisations had begun to snatch away workers...when many villages had lost one-third or even one-half of their able-bodied men...that the masses began to murmur.' The murmur soon became a roar.

Bloody Sunday, St Petersburg 1905

On Sunday 9 January 1905 a priest, Father Gapon, led a vast crowd of Petrograd (*now St Petersburg*) workers to present a reform petition to the Tsar. It was respectful enough in tone. It began: 'Sire, We workers, our children and wives, the helpless old people who are our parents, have come to you, Sire, to seek justice and protection.'

'People wore their Sunday clothes,' Trotsky recorded. 'In some parts of the city they carried icons and church banners... The march was a peaceful one, without songs or speeches.'

Instead of justice and protection they got bullets. In the great square before the Winter Palace 'a bugle sounded and the troops opened fire. The killed and wounded fell in hundreds. The crowd was so dense that the fire could not miss its mark.'

Bloody Sunday taught the workers the value of petitions to the Tsar. A tremendous wave of strikes, part political, part economic, swept the country from end to end.

They were led by rank and file militants and, since free trade unions had been illegal, improvised organisations were created.

It was in the textile town of Ivanovo-Vosnesensk that a great advance was made in May, 'the first Soviet of Workers' Delegates was formed'. The idea spread like wildfire. Soviets sprung up all over Russia. In June the sailors of the battleship Prince Potemkin of Taurus, the latest and most powerful ship of the Black Sea fleet, mutinied and threw out their officers.

This was the critical point. Trotsky wrote at the time 'a [political] strike brings the army of the revolution to its feet [but] the power still has to be snatched from the hands of the old rulers... A general strike only creates the necessary preconditions; it is quite inadequate for the task itself...

'The army stands in the way... At a certain moment in revolution the crucial question becomes on which side are the soldiers?'

Lenin put it more succinctly: 'That the people may rise and triumph over an army that remains loyal to the government is an absurd illusion,' he wrote.

In the event, the Potemkin mutineers remained isolated. The army, which consisted mostly of peasant soldiers led by predominantly noble officers, remained loyal to the Tsar.

Though the revolutionary movement continued to gather strength in the cities, culminating in a general strike in October, the badly-shaken Tsarist government retained the decisive weapon, control of the armed forces.

The Bolshevik-dominated Moscow Soviet organised an armed rising in December but after a week of fighting it was crushed. Though sporadic fighting continued into the new year in Russian controlled Poland, Finland and the

Baltic states as well as in the Caucasus, slowly but surely the Tsarist forces stamped out the rebels' units.

The reaction was savage. Military courts handed out 5,000 death sentences. Anti-Jewish pogroms, a speciality of Tsardom, swept the Western borderlands of the empire in which a majority of the world's Jews still lived.

The naked face of Tsarism was slightly concealed behind a 'constitution' which Tsar Nicholas had been forced to concede at the height of the Revolution, but the reality of despotism remained.

The socialist organisations were decimated and driven back underground. The Bolsheviks survived best. It was in this period of reaction that the differences between them and the other groups became fully developed.

During 1905 all the socialist organisations had put forward the slogan for a democratic republic. The Bolsheviks maintained that it could be achieved only by an alliance between workers and peasants, the 'liberal' representatives of capitalism would be on the other side.

The Mensheviks, Bundists and other rightward-moving groups relied on the co-operation of the liberals and came more and more to fear the consequences of working-class and peasant revolt.

The split took a particular form in Russia but it was part of an international development. In France, in Germany, in Italy, Britain and the Austrian Empire, it was becoming clear that the right wing of the rapidly growing socialist parties was in reality pro-capitalist.

It was not yet so apparent that the centre, the majority was revolutionary only in words. When, in 1914, the First World War revealed the truth, the Russian Bolsheviks were already a separate, genuinely revolutionary organisation.

Part 9:
RUSSIA ON THE BRINK...

'TO THE MARXIST,' WROTE LENIN IN 1915, 'it is indisputable that a revolution is impossible without a revolutionary situation; furthermore it is not every revolutionary situation that leads to a revolution... For a revolution to take place it is usually insufficient for the lower classes not to want to live in the old way; it is also necessary that the upper classes should be unable to live in the old way...

'Revolution arises only out of a situation in which the above mentioned objective changes are accompanied by a subjective change, namely the ability of the revolutionary class to take revolutionary mass action strong enough to break (or dislocate) the old government which never, not even in a period of crisis, 'falls if it is not toppled over.'

By early 1917 these conditions had not been met in Russia. The Tsar had entered into a system of military alliances with the 'democratic republican' government of the French Empire and the 'constitutional monarchy' of the British Empire against the German and Austrian empires.

Inevitably this alliance, and its counterpart on the German-Austrian-Turkish side, led to war. The war which started in August 1914, was, in Lenin's words, 'a bourgeois imperialist and dynastic war. A struggle for markets and for freedom to beat foreign countries,...a war to deceive, disunite and slaughter the working peoples of all countries by setting the wage slaves of one nation against those of another so as to benefit the capitalist bosses.'

It was also a war that made unprecedented demands on the economies of the warring countries. The Russian economy was too weak to bear that burden.

'The lack of munitions, the small number of factories for their production, the sparseness of railway lines...soon translated the backwardness of Russia into the familiar language of defeat... About fifteen million men were mobilised... About five and a half million were counted as killed, wounded or captured...approximately two and a half million killed.'

In the cities food shortages, shortages of clothing, of fuel, of all the necessities of life grew worse and worse – for the poor. The rich, glutted with war profits, feasted while cold, hungry workers slaved away for ten, twelve or fourteen hours a day.

In the factories and the army, the influence of the illegal socialist organisations, mainly Bolsheviks, began to grow rapidly. Yet even they did not yet understand how rotten the regime had become, how easily it could be overthrown. The initiative came from the women textile workers of Petrograd.

'The 23rd of February 1917 was International Women's Day. The social-democratic circles had intended... meetings, speeches, leaflets,' recorded Trotsky in his *History of the Russian Revolution*. 'It had not occurred to anyone that it might become the first day of the revolution. Not a single organisation called for strikes on that day.'

In spite of this, the women came out demanding bread from the authorities, 'like demanding milk from a he-goat,' wrote Trotsky. The strikers appealed to the Bolshevik-led metal workers to support them.

'We agreed to this with reluctance,' one of the local Bolshevik leaders remembered. Reluctance, because they expected the movement to be quickly defeated. 'It was taken for granted that in case of demonstration the soldiers would be brought out into the streets against the workers.'

About 90,000 workers came out on the 23rd and the women besieged the town hall. There was no shooting. Though the strikers did not yet know it, the Tsarist officials were afraid that the infantry would not obey orders to shoot the workers.

They were kept in their barracks. Next day the movement spread.

'About half of the industrial workers of Petrograd are on strike on the 24th...The slogan 'Bread' is obscured by louder slogans: 'Down with autocracy', 'Down with the war'...compact masses of workmen singing revolutionary songs.'

The government brought out its most reliable soldiers, the Cossack cavalry, who were better paid and more privileged than ordinary troops. They did not mutiny but they did not do what was expected of them either.

International Women's Day 1917, St Petersburg

'The Cossacks charged repeatedly, but without ferocity... The mass of the demonstrators would part to let them through and close up again. There was no fear in the crowd. The Cossack's promise not to shoot passed from mouth to mouth... Toward the police the crowd showed ferocious hatred... twenty-eight policemen were killed.' Still the soldiers did not fire.

The government had elaborate plans to put down 'disorder', based on its experience in 1905. It had 150,000 troops in and around Petrograd.

'The difficulty lay not in lack of foresight, nor defects of the plan itself, but in the human material.' By early 1917 the Tsarist army was almost as disaffected as the workers.

On the third day there were a quarter of a million workers on the streets and the government was forced to bring out the infantry. There was some shooting but not much.

Fraternisation between soldiers and workers went hand in hand with a systematic attack on the police. 'Soon the police disappear altogether.' The Bolshevik committee called for unlimited national strike. And the army was cracking.

'The soldiers of the Volynsky regiment were the first to revolt...its commander was killed.' The Litovsky and Preobrazhensky regiments followed. The 27th was the decisive day.

'Military revolt had become epidemic...Towards evening the Semonovsky regiment, notorious for its brutality in putting down the Moscow rising of 1905, came over to the workers...The Tsarist garrison of the capital, numbering 150,000 men, was dwindling, melting, disappearing. By night it no longer existed.' Two days later Tsar Nicolas abdicated.

But, who was in power? The workers of Petrograd and the soldiers of the garrison had made the revolution. A Petrograd 'Soviet of Workers' Deputies' sprung up at once and soon workers soviets, soldiers soviets, and, later, peasant soviets sprang up all over Russia.

In those first days after the fall of the Tsar effective power was in their hands. The old state machine had been destroyed.

However, the leadership of the important soviets was predominantly in the hands of Mensheviks and representatives of the peasant party, the Socialist Revolutionaries. For them, the object of the Revolution was a democratic, capitalist republic.

The workers must not take power, because Russia is not

ripe for socialism and since the workers' representatives are in fact in power they must hand over as soon as possible to the liberal representatives of capitalism.

They hastened to support a 'Provisional government' under a Tsarist nobleman, Prince Lvov, which had been cobbled together out of members of the Duma, the fake parliament set up after 1905. This government had no serious basis of support except that of the soviet leaders. This support was willingly given and, for the time being, it was enough.

Of course the 'liberals', were above all concerned to 'restore order', to re-establish the power of the officers over the soldiers and of the factory management over the workers. They were even anxious to retain a Tsar, not of course the discredited Nicolas, but a new face.

And they were determined to carry on the war with all the sacrifices by the ordinary people that this entailed. Russian imperialism was as important to them as to any Tsar.

And the Poles, the Finns, the Baltic peoples, the Caucasian peoples and the peoples of Central Asia must continue to submit to the rule of Mother Russia, who knows best. There can be no question of independence. Later perhaps, there can be discussion about some limited home rule.

Later perhaps! This became the constant refrain of the Provisional government and its 'socialist' supporters. 'We must wait for the election of the Constituent Assembly,' said the Menshevik leaders of the soviets. When will it be elected? Later.

Meanwhile order must be restored, the war must go on. Having put the capitalist liberals in power, the Mensheviks then went on to adopt their policies.

On 3 April Lenin arrived from Switzerland. A deputation of 'moderate' soviet leaders went to meet him. Its leader Cheidze made an empty speech about democracy.

Having turned completely away from the delegation, Lenin addressed the crowd. 'The hour is not far off when the people will turn their weapons against the capitalist exploiters.'

It was a declaration of war. The revolution, for Lenin, had only just begun.

Part 10:
RED OCTOBER!

'THE BASIC QUESTION OF EVERY REVOLUTION.' wrote Lenin in April 1917, 'is that of state power... The highly remarkable feature of our revolution is that it has brought about a dual power...

'What is this dual power? Alongside the Provisional government, the government of the bourgeoisie (capitalist class), another government has arisen...the Soviets of Workers' and Soldiers' Deputies...a power directly based on revolutionary seizure, on the direct initiative of the people from below, and not on a law enacted by a centralised state power... This power is of the same type as the Paris Commune of 1871.'

A situation of dual power cannot, in the nature of the case, be a stable state of affairs. You cannot combine a Paris Commune with a centralised capitalist government.

One side or the other must give way or be smashed. Which one?

The Provisional government was weak. It existed on sufferance, because it was tolerated, indeed supported, by the majority of the leaders of the Soviets.

These Mensheviks (social-democrats we would call them today) and leaders of the peasant party (Socialist Revolutionaries) stood for a capitalist republic. In the long run that must mean the end of the Soviets.

The Bolsheviks stood for, in Lenin's words, 'Not a parliamentary republic – to return to a parliamentary republic would be a retrograde step – but a republic of Soviets of Workers', Agricultural Labourers' and Peasants' Deputies throughout the country, from top to bottom.'

The great problem was to win a majority in the Soviets for a Soviet Republic. 'The class conscious workers must win a majority to their side. As long as no violence is used against the people there is no other road to power,' Lenin said.

Petrograd Soviet of Workers and Soldiers Deputies in session 1917

'We are not Blanquists, we do not stand for the seizure of power by a minority.' (Blanqui was a nineteenth century French revolutionary who advocated the capture of power by a small group of armed conspirators.)

Meanwhile the Provisional government and its 'socialist' backers were determined to carry on the war that was bleeding the country to death. The economic situation went from bad to worse.

The American socialist journalist, John Reed, described what he saw: 'On the freezing front miserable armies continued to starve and die without enthusiasm. The railways were breaking down, food lessening, factories closing.

'The desperate masses cried out that the bourgeoisie was sabotaging the life of the people... A large section of the propertied classes preferred the Germans to the Revolution – even to the Provisional Government...

'The speculators took advantage of the universal disorganisation to pile up fortunes... Foodstuffs and fuel were hoarded or secretly sent out of the country to Sweden... Week by week food became scarcer.'

A prominent Russian capitalist, Lianozov, told Reed: 'Starvation and defeat may bring the Russian people to their senses.'

And if not? 'Revolution is a sickness. Sooner or later the foreign powers must intervene here as one would intervene to cure a sick child.'

Naturally the Lianozovs were foremost in denouncing the Bolsheviks as unpatriotic and Lenin as a German agent!

Peace

The Bolshevik slogans were 'Peace, Land and Bread' and 'All Power to the Soviets'. On 18 April the Provisional government sent a note to the governments of Britain and France, assuring them that Russia would in no case make a separate peace.

It provoked a massive armed demonstration in Petrograd, supported by soldiers of the garrison and sailors of the Baltic fleet.

'That army of 25,000 to 30,000 soldiers, which had come into the streets for a struggle with the prolongers of war, was quite strong enough to do away with a far stronger government than that of Prince Lvov.'

In fact the government was helpless. The intervention

of the 'socialist' leaders of the Soviet was required to persuade the demonstrators to disperse.

'The April days had unequivocally lifted the curtain on the impotence of the Provisional government, showing that it had no serious support in the capital,' Trotsky noted. Terrified, the ministers begged the Mensheviks and SR leaders to join the cabinet, to provide it with some credibility amongst the workers, soldiers and peasants.

They did. The reformists lent their influence, earned in some cases by long prison sentences under the Tsar, to bolster up a government whose aim was to stop the Revolution.

Gradually they lost support. At the beginning of June, at the first Congress of Soviets, the Menshevik-SR bloc still had a big majority and was able to set up a Central Executive Committee composed of its reliable supporters. But that same month saw a massive anti-war demonstration in Petrograd carrying predominantly Bolshevik slogans.

Early in July much more formidable demonstrations demanding 'All power to the Soviets' led to bloody clashes and a near insurrection in Petrograd. The Bolshevik leaders tried to control and check the movement.

Petrograd, they knew, was ready for the overthrow of the government but Russia was not yet ready. This line was badly received by many Bolshevik supporters. Necessary as it was, it produced a certain degree of demoralisation and a growth of support for anarchist groups.

The Provisional government saw its chance and struck back hard. In what Trotsky called 'the month of the great slander', a torrent of fabricated 'evidence' was produced to show that the Bolsheviks were agents of the German Kaiser, supported by German gold.

Reorganised under the 'socialist' Kerensky and with a would-be Russian Napoleon, Kornilov, as Commander-in-Chief, the government was temporarily strong enough to arrest Trotsky, Lunarcharsky and others on a charge of treason. Lenin and Zinoviev were forced to go into hiding.

The effect was short-lived. Soldiers continued to desert. Peasants were seizing the land. The economic situation continued to deteriorate.

Commander-in-Chief Kornilov planned a military coup. Late in August his troops began to march on Petrograd. Some, at least, of the ministers were in league with him.

The persecuted Bolsheviks threw all their weight into a temporary defence of the Kerensky government against Kornilov.

'At a night session of the military organisation of the Bolsheviks, participated in by delegates of numerous army detachments, it was decided to demand the arrest of all conspirators, to arm the workers and supply them with soldier instructors and to guarantee the defence of the capital.'

Power

Kornilov was beaten. A tremendous swing to the left followed. The Bolsheviks gained a majority in the Petrograd Soviet.

Moscow followed. Then city after city. Early in October the Bolshevik central committee decided that the time was now ripe. An armed insurrection was planned, to be carried out under the auspices of the Petrograd Soviet.

Amid rumours of another right-wing attempt at a coup, detachments of soldiers and armed workers took over Petrograd on 25 October in the name of Soviet power. There was practically no resistance.

Only the Winter Palace was defended for Kerensky. The second Soviet Congress – 'the most democratic of all parliaments in the world's history' – assembled at the Smolny Institute.

The Bolsheviks and their allies were a large majority. The dual power was at an end. The first workers' state on a national scale had been born.

REDWORDS ★ PAMPHETS

Paul Foot once declared, that the Haitian Revolution which erupted in 1791, was 'perhaps the most glorious victory of the oppressed over their oppressors in all history'. It was a world-historic event, an epic twelve year long black liberation struggle which abolished slavery for good in what was then the prized French sugar plantation colony of Saint Domingue. In 1804, the new nation of Haiti was born, the second post-colonial nation ever and the first independent black republic outside of Africa. In two characteristically brilliant lectures, delivered in 1978 and 1991 and published here for the first time, Paul Foot made an impassioned and compelling attempt to bring home to his audience some sense of the richness of the 'hidden history' of the Haitian Revolution. Through an inspired popularisation of C.L.R. James's classic work, The Black Jacobins, the lectures showed the emancipation of the enslaved was fought for and won by the enslaved themselves. Yet the lectures also outline the importance of the outstanding revolutionary leadership represented by Toussaint Louverture. There are few better possible introductions to the Haitian Revolution for anti-racists and anti-imperialists today than this powerful retelling of the story of the only successful slave revolt in history.

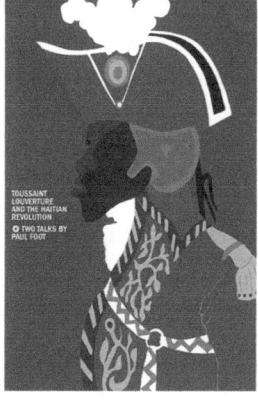

TOUSSAINT LOUVERTURE AND THE HAITIAN REVOLUTION
TWO TALKS BY PAUL FOOT

ISBN: 9 781914 143311

In 1871, the workers of Paris took control of the city. When they established the world's first workers' democracy, they found no blueprints or precedents for how to run their city without princes or politicians. As they built new institutions of collective power to overturn social and economic inequality, their former rulers sought to thwart their efforts. By noting the historic problems of the Commune, debates over its implications and the glimpse of a better world it provided, Gluckstein reveals its enduring lessons and inspiration for today's struggles.

The Paris Commune: A Revolution in Democracy
Donny Gluckstein

ISBN : 9781608461189
Harvester Press

When women workers' anger exploded onto the streets of Petrograd on International Women's Day in 1917, it lit a fuse that was to turn the world upside down. The centenary of 1917 is an opportunity to rediscover these momentous events, which changed the course of history and inspired generations of workers.

It toppled the Tsarist autocracy and hastened the end of the First World War and three other dynastic empires. The Russian Revolution proved another world is possible and showed how we might be able to win it. The workers and soldiers of Petrograd were the vanguard of the most important and the most successful social movement in world history. Women were at its forefront, tearing up the deep rooted oppression they faced. Today the deepening crisis of capitalism means a world in turmoil. Understanding 1917 and the movements and ideas that led to it is vital if we are to re-open the prospect of a better world before capitalism destroys the future.

Russia 1917: Workers' Revolution and the Festival of the Oppressed

Dave Sherry

ISBN : 9781910885406
Booksmarks Publications

bookmarksbookshop.co.uk

INDOMITABLE REVOLUTIONARY:
Duncan Hallas, A Tribute

Dave Sherry, Jack Robertson, Sheila McGregor,
Alex Callinicos, John Rudge, Laura Miles

ISBN : 9781914143724

bookmarks
the socialist bookshop
bookmarksbookshop.co.uk